Scavenging the Country
for a Heartbeat

Scavenging the Country for a Heartbeat

Poems by
Neil Shepard

1 9 9 2   F I R S T   P O E T R Y   S E R I E S

Mid-List Press   **Denver & Minneapolis**

Library of Congress Cataloging-in-Publication Data

Shepard, Neil, 1951-
    Scavenging the country for a heartbeat
        p. cm.—(1992 first poetry series)
    ISBN 0-922811-16-4 : $9.95
    I. Title. II. Series
PS3569.H39395S23 1993
811'.54—dc20   92-35765
                        CIP

Acknowledgements for previously published poems: *Antioch Review*, "The Bell Bird"; *Bellingham Review*, "The Mad Woman in Moonlight" (previously titled"One Night"); *Blueline*,"Late Spring at the Farm"; *The Blue Ox*,"Flesh"; *Chelsea*, "The Missing Ear"; *Denver Quarterly*, "Morning Composition"; *Kansas Quarterly*, "North Platte to Chicago, November Nights, Route 80"; *Mid-American Review*, "August in Ohio,""The Failing"; *Mickle Street Review*, "Waking Up, Losing Self"; *New Mexico Humanities Review*, "Testimony at Court House Rock"; *Nimrod*, "For Vivian," "After the Wishing Star Goes Down"; *North By Northeast*, "The Boy Who Was Part Frog"; *Poetry East*,"Mid-Winter Thaw, Vermont"; *Poetry Northwest*, "Anthem for the Disembodied"; *Poetry Now*, "The Double Bed"; *The Southern Review*, "Autumn at the Farm," "Atchafalaya November," "Astronomical," "Conviction"; *Tar River Poetry*, "Banding Bats"; *West Branch*, "Obedience."

For permission to use quotations we thank: James Baldwin's line used by arrangement with the James Baldwin Estate; lines from *The Summer Stargazer* by Robert Claiborne reprinted by permission of his estate, all rights reserved; lines from Paul Nelson's "Lobes" used with permission of the author; James Wright, "But Only Mine" from *St. Judas* © 1959 James Wright, Wesleyan University Press by permission of University Press of New England.

Manufactured in the USA

ACKNOWLEDGEMENTS

Special thanks to J.P. White who has read this book through numerous drafts and offered suggestions for its improvement. Thanks also to Bill Tremblay, Paul Nelson, Dan Tower, Mary Spagnol, Carolyn Gamble, Theresa Bacon, and Tony Whedon who, over the years, have helped me with these poems. Finally, thanks to Kate Riley who has given me the support and poetic suggestions I needed to see this book to completion.

I believe that the spiritual man must go back in order to go forward.

—Theodore Roethke, "An American Poet Introduces Himself"

CONTENTS

NOTES ON HUMAN EVOLUTION

CONVICTIONS

SCAVENGING THE COUNTRY
FOR A HEARTBEAT

NOTES ON HUMAN EVOLUTION

THE MISSING EAR

We know the left side belongs to the devil,
that he sits there in dusk, who was light,
whose loss of heaven gave us art.
　　　　　—Paul Nelson, "Lobes"

I put my good ear to the rail
where Lincoln's nose is squashed to a red cent.
Let my stunted one, slightly darker, grow to the light.
Any day, I can hear trembling
in the tracks, measure distance
by how loud the brassy chord
cuts the air. When it comes,
I can't hear Mother's warning,
nor Bach's chorale from the white steeple—
the one I played by heart
on the pink piano of the Children's Ward.
Even Father's car, stuttering
in the carport, unsteadily delivering me
to the depot, seems to lose its voice,
silenced as the crossing lights descend.

　　　　I remember winters of surgery,
wan doctors glossing their smooth fingers
over last year's scars, the tiny crosses
on my chest still red and hard.
And they said, *we'll lay another row*
of stitches here, little train tracks.
Little train tracks on the frontiers
of my life. Mother squeezed my hand
as the sonorous brass chorused around the curve
into Leominster, and we rode the Boston-Maine line
straight to the horizon.
　　　　　　　　And squeezed again
as she left the Children's ward
for South Station, and home. Then

the nurses poised above me like sails
to the land of the dead. Metal rails

3

of the gurney raised between us,
green ether-mask growing over my face,
and ether the color of sunlight,
and the silver bedpan strapped to my chin.
I battled my eyes open to damn white light,
two white-masked doctors cutting above me.
Flesh of my flesh, bone of my bone,
the ersatz ear was born. A lump of raspberry
shaped by unsteady hands. *In twenty years,*
we'll know enough to get it right.

I knew enough to carry myself
at an angle to light,
tilting my head as if
from the weight of white bandages.
I knew the sweet nothing of drugged sleep,
one fat pill every four hours
until I could not feel. The sobs inside
slurred their words, and slept.

And I awoke to twenty years
of sweet nothings: words whispered into an ear
denied meaning. Every lover whispered her separation.
Every friend's right-intending words drew blanks.
All those comic-strip balloons
with the words removed, and one actor
anxious to know his script. Words and words and words,

and yes and yes and little understood.
Go to your room, young man. Go to your room. And then music
where I could be lost from them, music
transported from bass to treble clef,
spun from the pressed grooves of records—
wordless music, Bach's balm on a bee sting
of the soul, unguent after pulling the deep splinter.
Music wove its inexorable way
to the left, the darker side, and healed
the cleft within me, transported my whole cranium
like a great station full of the music
of departure and arrival.

4

How then could I put *words* to music?
To sweeten the train's brassy song of separation?
Inside, I could hear perfectly.
Inside was as quiet as the velveteen
cushions of a Pullman car.
My twin inner ears tuned to the measure
of some nameless Other, some child-conductor
who mouthed the syllables of his separation.
Station by station as he pulled away,
he rode the parallel rails to the horizon
where they *seemed* to meet as one line.
He mused the sound of words
in perfect quietude, then choired
the voices of separation—
Mother, Father, abandoned one—
sotto voce to the void, and
chorale to the world, in unison.
I took an odd dictation.

      Until this morning, the light says *It is now.*
Mother and Father say, *the perfection of the ear*
has come. Time to be healed.
                And I hear myself
refuse the doctor's white hands, refuse
the scalpel that will slice the past from me
and splice some perfect-sounding future.
Something hard and perennial grows from me.
Something stunted, but swallowed and digested
as grief's memories: how many separations line the rails
when I touch the amulet of my ear.
How much light spills across these bandages,
mummified in the present. How much music
wails from the brass bull of my soul.
And still wrapped in swaddling bands,
something is born beautiful out of the missing—

a lifetime of anaesthetics, now one indefinite
article away, one article of faith away, from an aesthetic:
    What is missing
    makes memory whole.

THE DOUBLE BED

Brother, do you remember
how the sheets were sticky with mist,
the smell of kelp so close we were floating
on a bed of it; how if we listened well
we could hear a captain swearing the dark
at his drunken men, and the voices of women
laughing low over the street? Laughing
until they had passed from hearing
and still we heard them in the inner ear,
as teasing as the whispers
in the hollow of the conch.

Soon you would be struggling in your sleep,
your legs tangling with mine as the bed creaked.
It was perfect the way our legs locked
and did not draw back beneath the sheets
as they would now, as we imagine them now, when we speak.
We were restless for the clear morning.
If the kitchen light spilled into our room,
the pine-knots on the ceiling might become
buoys, fishing boats, tatoos.
You were three years younger, perhaps
never shared these thoughts, but those voices
breathing in from the street, do you remember,
were low, and salty with language.

THE MAD WOMAN IN MOONLIGHT

One night the crescent beach woke from my dream—
a perfect derriere curve, waves ribbed like French
ticklers, all under the exposed breast of a moon—

and the one mad woman in moonlight I had dreamed
for ten years, wrapped in the tippet of night sea,
lonely for her lover lowered in a sub,
periscope up, torpedo fired into the surf—

she was there, toeing the water's edge, sifting shells
in the runnels of what washes up and returns.
Bon soir she said, and however it was, we dawdled
down the strand to darkness far from amusement lights.
At twenty, my life more precious

than the sheathed knife strapped to her thigh
only a woman of moonlight would carry,
I bid her adieu, in the phony French whisper

of waves, adieu to the g-string I might worry
from beneath her clothes until it was taut
as piano wire across my throat. Adieu, adieu,
as Sidney Bechet's whole notes, *April in Paris*,

floated out from screen-porch parties,
gulled across the moonlight
to search the garbage dumps of love.

And along the bulkhead, my two cousins,
staggering, beer-breathed, crooning *Moon River*,
fell to either side, into shadows where they fired
dream-fusillade into their loving hands. I joined them

for love's weak-kneed appointment, moaned how romance
is all blood and daggers
before the last gasp. We felt the moon's gibbous curve

more like a pita-pocket, the crescent beach
more like a stuffed croissant, and waves an effervescence

we might find bubbling up from any fast food stand.
Suddenly hungry, we stalked toward the rollercoaster lights.

As for the mad woman in moonlight, I learned
she was a third cousin the next afternoon.
She held no particular fascination.

FLESH

Driving on the road South
I imagine leaving the cave
of your body, but a thousand
side-passages lead me deeper.
You ask for more dirt, and I admit
I like the taste of it too.
There's great unholiness in eating.

Past Nashville we stop at a motel,
slip quarters into the wall and feel
our bed full of the rhythm of other rooms,
the whole foundation shaken in sweat.

*

You take the wheel in Tuscaloosa.
Noon is so humid
I give up on my body and lift
toward the shadow of leaves
alive with cicadas. They molt
from their old skins and *chee-ee* with delight.

So this is what it's like
to leave the body: we arrive naked
with *another* one. Half-here,
I sense you drifting beside me,
loosening your grip on the steering wheel.
Have you already lifted out,
gone on ahead to New Orleans?

Earlier you imagined grille-work on the villas
delicate as tatting, flowering honeysuckle
drugging the senses.
When we arrive it will be that
and streets steaming with jambalaya, red beans and dirty rice,
the shrill horns of Bourbon Street
gyrating a g-string.

*

9

Stuffed full of French pastries
we laze along the river-walk,
breathing the last waters of the Mississippi
emptying into the Gulf.
Here, where fresh water turns salt,
we are, like Lot's wife, stunned
by the sheer weight of our senses.
You tuck your head under my arm
and we are one tranced hen,
lacking even the dream of flight.

All the muddy headwaters of the Mississippi
end here, turbulent as sweat, not yet
given in to the final form of brine.
I want to stay here longer,
but the wind whips us one way or the other.

*

I consider driving on alone
past Pointe a la Hache, Port Sulphur, to Blind Bay.
No more leaves swollen with dust.
Always warm rains. Chiggers and botflies.
Every warm-blooded thing itching
to get out of its skin.

The sun tangles in branches as it comes down
and brings me back to you, your eyes green as leaves
gracing the gray limbs. Together, we watch the swallows
circle a few times before coming down.

AUTUMN AT THE FARM

All August it was hot with our voices.
But tonight, as autumn comes out of Canada,
we stand under the stars searching meteors.
This is one game we still play: both seeking
the same brief fires in the dark.

If we could only remain here quiet,
let the universe expand without us . . .
But even as I hold you
I can feel the cool amethyst,
ringed on your finger, the stone of your birth,
pulling away.

You will return to the tropics
to work the mist-nets along the flyways,
to sack the bats in the fatal air of guano caves.
At this, I want to hug you to me.
I can't remember the last time I loved you
for your own choices. And so you go.

All summer I sweated to make things grow.
Yet as fall comes on, I watch the mulberries droop,
fat with magic. Birds peck them and disappear
into the far air.
Perhaps following the flyway south, perhaps returning.
I have only questions.
Yesterday the yellow poplar bloomed
its once in eight years.
Is this the wages of patience?

I try to believe.
But morning after morning,
the cardinal beats his wings against our bedroom window,
calling a clipped warning: *chit, chit.*
In this I hear my father's prayers unanswered:
be fruitful and multiply.
The mourning dove sings like wind through wire
and our clothes flap at odds on the line.

Still they are drying, growing lighter in the growing dark,
emptied of our bodies.
And so we stand beside them, catching chill,
as the wind comes faster now out of the north.

NOTES ON HUMAN EVOLUTION

All day, illusion and disillusion:
the museum full of stuffed life,
and skeletons set right with the glue
of boiled horse. All day,
I've watched her hands guide the bones
of an Old World beast back to form.

I can't remember the last time she touched me
with that much care. Like a dead man rising
from troubled earth, I remember being
unable to breathe beneath her hair,
she on top, burying the small bones.

I wander through rooms of Peruvian totems—
the lizard of fertility plastered
to a woman's hair; the wise native
with the lying fox stuck to his beard—
and feel again how the past is lost.

She busies herself on the top floor,
now piecing the tiny bones together,
now polishing the glass eye of a wolf
to a shine pure as spirit.

But looking into his fixed eyes,
I remember my own dog, stiff with too many hours
of highway death. As I carried him in my arms,
I believed then his eyes were bright
looking into the other world.

CARLETON'S HILL

This time I come home with a bride.
And as ritual has it,
we go to Carleton's Pond.
But the years have hedged
and hemmed it in—stands of bramble,
straggling trees with wrist-thick vines.
The pond itself reduced to a watering hole
for shrews, shrikes, and a few odd ducks.

I show her the place sunfish struck,
and we watch a few tadpoles waggle off.
Much of the pond is muck, tepid pools
destined to crack with summer mud.
She giggles when I say it's spring-fed,
so I go to find the proof again.
When I was ten, with an ear to the ground,
I followed the sound of water splashing
under rock, uphill, along a bowled-over
stone wall, to the trunk of a black walnut.
And there the water spurted up,
the legendary walnut from which all waters flow.

This day, we hear nothing beneath us.
I trace the trail far up,
but the walnut must have been cut.
We crawl now through thickets,
sweat to reach a stump or stone I can recall.
We scatter rabbits and wrens in their nests,
scare up ruffed grouse in a rush of wings
we hear as our own hearts pounding,
flushed from dead-ends.

She laughs at the looks of us,
scratched and bleeding, stained with berries,
and I join in the momentary laughter of loss.
So we manage to the top of Carleton's Hill,
still plowed for a view each summer.
Though I can no longer spot the small world

of the pond hidden in tall brush,
I can see far off: past eighteen
long fairways, sprawling suburbs, to the last
stone-walled pastures, and beyond, to roads rising
all the way to the hills of New Hampshire.

I trace each new view with her, and reckon my losses
against the wide horizon.
If it can be reconciled—this loss
of wild ramblings, ponds teeming
a full nature—it is here
at the top of Carleton's Hill
where I turn my gaze a full circle
and see the distances still stretching away.

SUBURBAN MEDITATION

Moon shines silver
on the window-lock—
girlish curves clasped
to the safety of a catch.

My new wife
hugs to her pillow,
down deep in dreams.
She doesn't hear me open
the window, breathe the thieving night.

Out there, one red star
keeps its sheen beside the moon.
It strikes flint in a sky
all silver-flecked,
and does not fade.

Silver the sky,
and silver the shadeless rooms
of this new home,
silver the bowls and flatware,
the fine china of Staffordshire,

silver my parents' anniversary
who have taught me to live
too easily
with this dying heart

as the roof of marriage
closes over. Or is it
the "lintel" of marriage
opening to a new branch?

Either way, there's the catch—
something dimmed with the moon's silver arrows
and these silver rooms—perhaps the last stag
of the forest.

16

Who wouldn't want to flee
into the sanguine night—
these houses earshot to earshot,
old women chirping like house sparrows
Mahjong, Mahjong, through the screens.
All the dull geometry of carpentry,
inside and out.
                              There goes the red star
angling above a neighboring roof.

I can see the sad faces of romance
floating from TV screens,
their images spilling silver-blue
across the neighboring lawns.
We come to silver by degrees,
silver the wedding ware,
and finally silver-haired,

as with these old husbands
muttering their incantations to the screen,
which alchemize this endless night
to earth-bound August.

Of course, they too must have had nights
when darkness stole in,
and seen the red star near the moon,
as tonight, rising
above the neighboring roof,

rising above the tired antenna
of all false romance,
above phone wires that held
all love borne of longing in their thin arms,

rising, even, above the eaves of their own vision,

until they pulled away from the opened window
and it burned on, alone,
to the center of the sky.

MORNING COMPOSITION

A turning fan, set in the window of a summer's morning,
turned the air all night from darkness into light,
turns me now to my wife's, my own turning forms.
Air moves over our bodies, moves itself invisibly
toward dissolution. We are more visible.
I see my wife's thin shoulder, the rudder
that guides us sleeping into the port
of another day. We wake to darkening bays
circling our eyes, harbors creaking and groaning
for each new odyssey. The mortal condition
bellies our sails and the sculpted goddess
blessing our journeys from the bow
begins to weather. Our own forms swell—
a new puffiness of eyes *here*, this morning,
a new wrinkle *here*, a new
network of protruding veins strapping the anklebone
for the long haul. The rheumy eye opening
to this morning, by a trick of vision,
blurs the moving fan to distinction—
each thin blade, separated by the space of an instant,
chops the air as it makes its rounds
in the wards of time,
announcing itself as *now*
and *now*.

THE ENIGMA

All day you drift
through the house like a cloud
trying to remember
the feeling of brightness behind you,
warmth at your back. You're gray
and distant, indistinct to yourself.
What precipitates this mood?
As troubled air gathers itself
in an updraft, so in the vacuum
you've created, you gather the evidence:
yesterday's dishes still undone, egg stained
to the plate, milk fogging the glass.
Clothes from every season scattered
on the floor like an action
painting; maps opened and red-penciled
like so many bleeding veins
in the geography of departure. A slight
rumbling comes from somewhere other
than the belly: an occluded cold front
undercuts the memory of morning warmth.
Her slightly musty smell's dispersed
by bathroom disinfectant. Your phone
machine blinks off and on. Rewind
and her voice sounds strong, vaguely
familiar as if you could trace it
through tissue paper. What form
will you take now that the house is dark
around you? Will you harden into hail, hardball size,
or risk a gentle rain, a warm,
wet letting go? Either way, a sudden
shaft of light pierces through: she's gone.
You're the last to know.

EASTER AT WHEDONS'

for Tony and Suzanne

Digging for Jerusalem artichoke
and horseradish root in a sunlit patch
where spring snows have melted clear.
The earth soft for the taking,
I dig down here because the pain
has not stopped, has buried me
in a drifting, white uncertainty,
a swirl that rages and does not die,

until I cannot live another minute
with Millet's "Laughing Girls"
half-veiled in the shadows of my home,
giggling into courtyards full of light
to whatever suitors wave beyond the frame;
cannot live with the wandering Jew
tangled in a brown mat of neglect,
the jade jaded with a surfeit of sun,
and the home and family I had dreamed
with her, gone.

                       I come to Whedons' house
because they will not have me Easter alone.
Hours ago, we soaked salt from the ham,
scalloped potatoes, baked bread
we will break together in another hour—
and then off to dig these offerings,
roots and tubers fresh from winter.

We walk their twenty acres,
rehearsing this season of plenty—
mark the hummocks and brooks rising,
the moss rising and the bog rising,
tadpoles and water beetle swelling,
the white larvae too numerous to count
swelling like stars in a dark pool.
I eat the root in my hand until the water

of my eyes is confused and pain has suddenly a taste.
I gnaw at tubers, dirt and all,
their buttery, nutty flavor that heals
the tongue of its wounds,
the flavor of having lasted
all winter beneath the earth, under the good graces
of the snows, under death's small matter
of leaves and grasses. And still whole
at the next turning of the earth.
I cradle these roots in my hands,
note the blood from digging, blood
under my nails, in the creases
of my marrying lines, along the knuckles
scraped raw.
                              To the berry bushes
returning with their red scars and bulges,
we do a sun-old dance. We test
the winter-surviving timbers
that will rise in a new wood shed;
spin the water wheel that with snowmelt
will generate its one watt of light.
And we rehearse the divorce
to come—how I will swallow whatever grief
has ham as its first salt-washed course,
and bitter herbs, and bread broken
from the whole loaf with friends.

Night in their cabin, we listen
to the waters curling around the foundation,
small waterfalls stumbling among the stones,
sacring bells of sound to wash pain
smooth as silt. Evening rumbles from the west,
thunderheads worrying a path across the sloping dell
until we imagine by the fire-lit last course
of dinner how our cabin is an ark,
with its kerosene lanterns swinging port and starboard,
its pairs of dogs and cats, its couple of proprietors,
and their one guest casting for an olive branch,
as we float down the swale to Route 118,
past surrounding towns—Jericho, Jerusalem—
clear to the heart of Montgomery Center.

MID-WINTER THAW, VERMONT:
A VISIT FROM MY WIFE

Since she is coming
and she will be cold
even on a winter day
when it soars to forty,
I go down to the woodpile
and pull up a few bottom logs.

With thaw, they've come unstuck,
uncased from the ice. There's unexpected
green beneath them, a stunned
green stuck to the bark's puzzling design.

When she comes, the sun
will start again toward a dipping hour,
our love continue its descent
into bittersweet friendship.
We might even lie together
 in the sleep of the long settled,
might feed off the fat of some sweetness
we tasted together in the past,

before an avalanche drops from a bough,
icicles melt clear to extinction,
and whatever new green is coming, comes.

EX'S

We're driving west, putting distance between ourselves
and the newest crop of lost loves. What can be worse
than two jilted lovers, watching the horizon together

as sun slides into the world, behind our backs,
exposing the furrows of our pain.
You could say we're driving toward more pain

and you'd be right. But what did we know, what
do we ever know when we're hurt except the need
for its cessation. For the moment, distance

seems to soothe like time. Two thousand miles
from my ex is a long ribbon of highway to forget
her hair. And two thousand miles makes Carolyn forget

her ex's supple spine. I watch her perfect legs
fold and unfold across the vinyl seat, she watches
my sleek arms. We agree the seats are hot,

the light transforms a few silhouettes of trees
into the nape of my ex's neck or the small
of her ex's back. You see how confused it gets.

For a few days, we might hold each other
against a cut-out sky, the cottony clouds pasted on.
We might drink from each other's bodies

as in the old days between us when rain at one's lips
reminded the other of thirst. But we know we'll fail,
as all unhealed things fail. The flattened sun

slides on its string of light. A few wisp clouds,
squeezed of moisture, are lost in enormous blue.

THE YEAR OF HALLEY'S COMET

The year of Halley's Comet
my wife grew indistinct.
Other women's faces mooned in mine—
luminous promise swirled out of the dark
inner spaces and into view.
In my first unlovely winter
love came to nothing, a few dirty
snowballs tossed in jest across
the enormity of all we had already been—
blazing selves galvanized to the circling
roles of husbands and wives, mothers
and fathers, blazing until our essence
burned down to the cinders and ice
of genealogy.

The year of Halley's Comet
the gravity and density of old
affairs, unfinished lives, old dust
and ice, impacted to a hard center.
Old grievances nicked my face
like grains of burning ice.

I flew South for warmth and a clear view
of the comet's tail. But each coral key
was a flash of memory, a point of light
where we'd danced at the coquina bars.
At route's end, the place where the last
key unlocks the door and the sun
passes through, I saw exotic birds—
white ibises and roseate spoonbills—
as common as pigeons on the streets.
They refused the magnificence of their swoopings
and wheelings that set the sky ablaze. . .
for the convenience of pecking crumbs
on the streets of Key West.

On those streets, I remember only the women's faces
I could not approach, brightened with desire

and then fuzzed, snowed, cancelled out
the minute the old solitary pull took us again
to the edge of the world we had made in our coming.

Yes I might have saved a few faces,
taken home to dream, and used them
in my private ways, but by then,
they were my own face, made of my
bones and sorry exhalations.

That winter I rose at five
to witness Halley's Comet pass
across our galaxy, to see its tail
of ice and dust tell us who we are.
What I saw seemed frozen in place,
fuzzy and indistinct, this once
in a lifetime, after all,
a disappointment.

AFTER LOVE

As you leave me, memory
by memory, the petals drop
and the dark center remains—
loves me, loves me not.

I remember first your thirst for water,
your mouth immersed in mountain streams,
your long body submerged in Snowmass Lake
for as long as the stifled scream of being
could hold. I rubbed the numbness from you,
made roses of your flesh.

                              At Buckskin Pass,
you rolled in wildflowers while I named them—
bluebell, forget-me-not, monkshood—
pressing them like premonitions
in the book of memories.

Later, in Louisiana,
we witnessed the bloom of spoonbills
roseate in sunset, lifting off
from their roosts, and pink water pipits
scattering the last feather-fluff of their young,
prying the bulrush nest apart. By then,

you'd come three times under the knife,
each stitch in your breast a notched reckless-
ness, sending you down swampy corridors
of cypress stumps and scarred tupelo,
pursuing barred owls to their unknown ends,
while I backwatered and steered.

What were you after that last spring
the wetlands rose above their banks, above
the height of a man? In fitful photographs
we snapped for whom? for the world?—
some search party stumbling upon our hollowed
bones, party to snake and king vulture?—

in those photos, my head is a nimbus
of setting sun, your shoulders squared
to blue indifference, the swamp-mist
sinking behind us, sinking in the graininess
of our bodies, in our clouded eyes.

Were some latter-day searcher
to find these photo-blooms of memory,
would he have seen desperation in your
dogged paddling, thrusting a handle down
to touch the gator's snout? Would he have smelled
the last traces of your leaving? Seen the corona
as your shadow eclipsed you? Would he have foreseen

the bluebell falling from the flowerbook,
the fine dust of forget-me-not
betraying me back to that first
wild field where you rolled in the soil.
Five years, and I am that man

who leads the expedition back, who floats above
the fields of monkshood, above
our old pirogue drifting in a dead-end
inlet, our bones bleached easy now
on the gunwales, so brilliant
in sunlight they are black.

CONVICTIONS

TWO DEATHS AND A TRANSMIGRATION

I hugged her when she returned.

Hugged her as. . .
as I had not hugged my wife in years.

"I scattered his ashes today,"
she said. "They scattered into sandpipers
flitting down the beach. The sandpipers,

I mean, scattered down the beach,
rose like ash and scattered,

their shadows under them,
then flew into them, and alit on land."

"I'm sorry," I said. "It must have been like. . . "

" . . .letting go," she said. "The sand took my tears.

The way those sanderlings lived with the waves,
pecking death from the ebb-tide
plucking their morsels up to flood-tide—

a shoreline, you might say,
defined each time
by where they came to rest."

"Anything I say sounds hollow," I said.
"Even grief is a platitude."

To which we hugged again
as I had not hugged my wife. . .

"Nothing is like anything else," I said.
"His loss must be inconsolable."

"His ashes scattered into sandpipers," she said.

"He flew over the ocean and returned."

AUGUST IN OHIO

Lean out a window any evening,
you can follow it—
the great gray clouds
drifting back into a grayer place.

The change is so soft and gradual.
Let all you can remember of loss
waste away in the Ohio haze,
blending day into night so easily
you'll hardly feel fear or
fear feeling as the air
grays a darker shade.

Whatever is in your heart of contention,
let the crickets sing it into twilight,
and be done with it. Grays can take you straight
in the moss-mist to sleeping. And by morning,
you too will drift awake, prepared for death after death.

LATE SPRING AT THE FARM

A garland of shadflies weaves overhead
dipping for blood, even these few dying hours.

What do any of us inherit but an end?
I've stripped down to nothing this noon,
hacked at bamboo shoots in the garden,
their wells of water spilling open
like the middle years of life.

They seem endless,
a skein threading the lawn and garden.
I can feel the muscles tighten under my skin
as I grip one root and pull.
Father never showed me the underside of soil.
He was firm
with his golf-game,
and I held the flag that signalled
the empty cup.

Oh, I could blame him more
if other hands were beside mine,
working the earth.
But the great middle years are greatly empty
in this house. The loon cries
the song of one beyond the marsh,
when the sky opens sideways long enough
for a winged-double to pass over.
Then it calls and calls.

Alone, I slip into a gravedigger's hunch
and keep hacking, hitting at the black mass
of roots disappearing into the earth.
Down this deep I hit slate
set here years ago to drain and aerate.
Someone old as this plot
hand-chiselled stone from the mountain
and brought it down.
So this is the magic

of corn breaking ground, knee-high by July.

This, the endless source of bamboo.
Too long I've neglected the work to be done:
the firm foundation, the lay of the land,
the humus and ash, the clusters of seeds,
the distance between, the rain, sun,
turn of the earth, the roots going down
to cradle a stone.

Too long I've neglected...

The small wings above me still hunger for another hour.

AFTER THE WISHING STAR GOES DOWN

Supper was sober tonight,
the talk sparse. We settled lightly
enough on the porch, but Trask
figured heavily the hail loss,
then retired early.

To sleep with nothing in our heads
but the turn of the earth, and the slow turn
of seed to stubble.... Trask stood in clover
this morning and said turn it under.
The first clouds came soon after.

Tomorrow I'll cancel the new combine
and hitch the horse. Trask will have to go.
The furrows in his brow knit nothing but worry.
I know the knot a man is
who faces labor without love.
Last month we feared dry soil,
so we planted barley
because we had to plant something.

When real rains came, he lay in bed.
I went out alone and found white roots
pushing down to drink rain, and sprouts
just topping the crust. Had he seen then.

Tonight I told him years back
this whole valley was nothing but dust.
He grunted, said, nothing's changed.
This hail fell hard. I saw birds
go down and cattle bruised.

So the barley's busted down to dross:
it'll make good pasture for now.
This storm will give us plenty
of wet for a new wheat crop.
Nothing comes to nothing, if the timing's right.
Stop turning it over and get some sleep.
The evening star is hours down over the hill.

MEDITATION AT CARLETON'S POND
(July, 1984)

> *As long as the water is troubled, it cannot become stagnant.*
> *—James Baldwin*

I

Thirty years ago, trees mirrored the stillness
of the frog pond. Every long hour
cowbells rung in the clover.

We circled the shore,
cast our lines for the anonymous bubble
breaking the surface, hooked and reeled in

blue gill or bass.
Every boy was happy with this.
We could hold a slippery moment

in our hands and toss it back
to keep the pond stocked,
the pull rippling the surface.

No one thought to slash the throat or gills,
breathe the water-bearing air of fish,
air of another movement that thrashed against the hook.

II

Ten years later, how heavily
the air hung with the solemn,
safe dreams of life. The pond

hung with a green scum,
blotting our faces on the shore.
We wondered who we were

as algal bloom rose fists
to the sky, blotting reflection,
swallowing all the air.

Fish flopped and stunk on shore,
their mouths open in indolent O's.
We cast about for clearer waters,

found more blemished pools—
the turbulent underbelly
thrashing its death-throes.

III

Then it was late sixties
and free-floating weeds
apostatized to solid masses,

new roots and tubers clutched
the pond's black bottom.
We burned the stars

and stripes in bonfires
built from brush-thickets
that overran the bridle path.

We burned all night
the low limbs of white pines,
sang protest songs as we ranged

over rye grasses, bowled over stone walls,
kicking private property to hell.
We were a groundswell, a force

of nature, unstoppable,
until Old Carleton stood his ground
with a shotgun. High on mescaline,

I visioned the skull-face of the future
in this pond—Old Carleton's grinning no—
and new trees shooting out through the holes

of his eyes, and the bonfire behind me,
now in the pond of his mouth, burning.

IV

I no longer find a path to the old pond
and, having bartered my own lone nature
for a few choruses of *We Shall Overcome*

sung with more fervour than peepers in new-summer,
I feel stricken when I return to the stone wall
now upended by tough vines and ivy,

small stands of birch and beech and wild pine.
What child today can find his way alone?
By instinct I know the direction,

but I'm scratched and shaken
when I stumble from the lea,
bloodied by briars and striving trees.

The very contour of the pond's bottom has changed,
and new, straggling limbs disturb its reflection.
No longer the towering elms' arched grace,

fan vaulting above the waters.

V

I can't fathom the pond turned swamp,
how trees took root in water,
how it reflects what I have lost:

a leanness of limb,
a growing in all directions at once,
a disregard for what has passed, is passing.

I find everything unfamiliar and ungoverned.
Though I too once grew wild in the weed-beds,
I learned the disciplined eye of solitude,

tracked deer to drinking water,
read the print of bobcat to its den,
and came upon, by evening, irenic hours of elm

bridging shadows in the water's darkening heaven.
Now breaking through bramble to the water's edge,
I find remnants of torn kites

snapped from the string of some child's hand
and fallen here, pierced
by the limbs of the least-wizened tree.

VI

The pond now mirrors its broken nature;
the search for the legendary walnut from which all waters flow
seems further away than ever. Now I might alter this seeking

to final things, to means and ends,
to the irrepressible thirst of the salt of the earth
for change, for a final drink at the waters of creation.

Yes, the trees are rising up around me
and here and there, weed and wildflower
shoot up uncompromisingly for their fair share of the world.

If I still lived in this town,
I might talk up restoration for the pond,
recall to the young men how Old Carleton

kept the pastures open, stocked the pond,
and granted us our wild youths on even tracts of land,
on well-worn paths through the woods.

Or would I will it wild as the green willow
now growing out of the old stump? How tangled it's all become.
And I fear for the youth which follows.

THE BOY WHO WAS PART FROG

Three years younger, he jumped when we said jump.
He returned with his father's trench coat,
a relic of real trenches, with pockets deep as its name.

Then we prodded him into the pond
with real sticks and stones
that loosed the cast-out spirit.

He dipped and swooped with a frenzy,
a bird or beast, clutching their green backs,
or turtling up to grab their white bellies.

He nabbed some by the crooked legs as they dove,
cupped others by their curious heads,
their gold-rimmed eyes just waking

from murky sleep, ready to believe anything
was another dark dream, ready to forgive anything
for a moment of light and air.

We applauded his finesse
as he tucked them into deep pockets
and inside flaps—the coat billowing

like a dark cloud about him, a shadow
that would pass over water.
Finally, he would trudge from the mud—

his feet webbed with pond weeds and sludge—
three frogs to a fist—a head here, a struggling leg there—
and frogs leaping from his pockets,

piggybacking into our greedy hands,
as he stood there sleek with scum,
twitching a little from the cold,

half-amused at our hurried thanks
as we went off to skin them alive,
his golden eyes ready to forgive us anything.

CONVICTION
(Brattleboro, 1899)

*Sundays were for baseball and God, and with due respect
to Him, in that order.*
—A History of Vermont

Blue laws bind them
to church and afternoons harmless with baseball.
These men in sepia tint, hair and whisker
seemingly still growing in the fading
daguerreotype . . . the pace is slow, untroubled
as their knowledge of God—
a bloop double, an error
chased without conviction,
but still it sends them easily
round the bases . . . the steeple
rising in the far outfield.
The days haze over,
batting Sunday afternoon into breeze,
and nowhere in their easy frames do they swing
with the savage knowledge of their yellowing.

little america

> August rest-stop, Nebraska,
before the onslaught of Fall.
Three a.m. we pitch in witchgrass,
an acre of *little america*
cut from the croplands.
At the edge of tent-sites,
high-tension wires hum,
some mega-farm shines its badge
from every hammered post.

> Nearby, semis whine in their sleep,
a trucker's stubbled face
pock-marked against plate glass,
his forehead contaminated green,
the miles of America glowing.
Diesel perfumes his sleep,
a wife waiting in the moist east.
Couples snuggle in camper vans,
their dreamwheels turning:
tomorrow and tomorrow, another thousand miles
comes the freedom. Make-shift awnings
shudder in a breeze like little pieces
of the Ritz.
> Crowns of wheat
nodding off, the kingdoms of summer almost lost,
but full now, full coffers of August.
By the wire fence, wheat leans over the edge—
blackened by current or ergot rot
feasting on the harvest.

> Where are the first-class travellers tonight?
In what Hyatt or Hilton do they bed down?
In what air-conditioned room, cool as the air
of Fall, do they unwrinkle and unruffle?
When they lay dollars in the fat hands
of bell-hops and bell-captains preening
in green uniforms, do they see
beyond their sparkling waters?

Do they dream of the serious, swollen
features of America, bruised and blackened, without
a vanishing cream or emollient?
                        How far away this tent-site
where we stake the meager soil.
Who *is* here in *little america*?
Chevy Chevette, no A/C, flat-out 60
at the speed limit. Winnebago and a blue TV
won on the elderly prayerwheel of America.
Volkswagen bus and bug, aging anarchists
rattling their rat-trap engines. And the young,
ersatz others who could become almost anyone.

        Someone cannot sleep tonight,
out relieving his dog.
Someone is queuing at the information booth,
readying his questions: how much
for a piece of dog heaven?
How much to holy Toledo?
What warranty on my dreamwheel?

        All night, radio towers burn and blink
their bleary cyclopic eyes, news and music
never enough to bridge the distance
between men and giants. One man,
impeccably dressed, his face forty feet high,
beckons us into his savings bank
from a billboard. Another giant,
his hands open in benediction,
offers life insurance in the forked lines
of his palms. Thousands of bugs
careen and crash against the lighted display.

        Pitched, taut, full of malevolent
wind, the tent bucks at its tether, and stays put.
The stakes have been raised from the ground.
Beneath us, quack grass. Above, plains lightning—
great chains of it rolling up and down the sky,
and for all that movement, there is no place to go.
We see the farthest expanse, see lightning

leaping to the horizon and back again:
and there is no rain.

                        Almost dawn,
bad breath and stubble erode
the waning moon. Barely real
at this hour, *little america*
like a cardboard cut-out
propped against the horizon.
The moon's scumbled beyond recognition,
blue beginning to show through.
A moon of chipped porcelain, impossible
as Rockwell's America, in the dawn sky,
sadly lost as the human figures
in Wyeth's enormous grasses—

           all of it leaning over the edge
toward flatbeds piled high with Port-O-Lets.
Where are they going tomorrow? To every half-built
high-rise, mall, and gentrified
quarter, that's where. Where every Tom, Dick, and Harry
can hammer his thumb, and have a pot to piss in.

POETRY

> *For we, which now behold these present days*
> *Have eyes to wonder, but lack tongues to praise.*
> —*William Shakespeare*, Sonnet 106

As I tighten a couplet the quarrel
shrills, strains my lilting rhythm past returning.
Strident cries of the dykes next door cut through the wall,
the single plywood sheet that keeps our marriage beds distinct.
I wonder what they mean by love, these butch bitches,
screaming "I love you, you bitch, you fuckin' cunt, I love you!"
to the stress of slamming doors. Something heavy smashes
the wall and breaks, and I rise up to yell for quiet.
    Each night they do something with dogs and music,
yipping and whining to acidic guitar till my wife calls for quiet
and they tell her to die.
Then I pummel the wall while they swear through the cracks.
Tonight my wife shushes me, her face pressed to the wall,
and we hear their misshapen rage raining fire:
    "I bust my ass three jobs swabbin' floors to rent this hole.
I come home and you're boozin' with the girls. Where you get off,
you and those fuckin' dykes?"
    "What's it to you? They give the shirts off their backs,
those girls. Where you get off bossin' my face..."
    "But I love you, you bitch, you fuckin' cunt, I love you."

    We listen through the wall to the rough strife
they tear, these amorous birds. What balls they have swearing
at four in the morning till the rooster tucks his head under wing
and refuses the sun's rising. Who is the fixed foot, who the compass
of this pair? Yes, one, the one who calls me dildo-face, cowers beneath layers
of rouge and false lashes, but her barbed tongue blasts this soft vision,
her Jersey slang banging against the back of my head until filth
is familiar as the brightest sprung rhythm.
And the other, who swore I'm paranormal-normal, the one like a dark wind
whirling back from the damned screams
"I love you, you cunt, love the shirt off your back!"
    Something heavy smashes the wall and breaks,
and I can almost see the awkward, fragile shape it takes
on our side of the duplex, can almost see gnarled passion taking aim,
shattering the old vessel that held the rose, and my wife with her thesis

44

and I with my tight couplets and slant rhymes spinning,
the words confused and climbing the borders of the page
as on the thermals of two private hells
until I must brace back the plywood and bark with the dogs
that I am dumb at the gates of such passion
and lack tongues to praise.

FOR VIVIAN

That afternoon, worn from the telling,
you slept as darkness came, and dreamed
your father's dream of command,
how he'd come in angry,
take your mother from peeling onions,
and slam the bedroom door.
Outside, snowclouds hung over the flag
and friends left for Germany, Tuscany,
with bad luck, Korea. When a boyfriend left,
you touched your tongue to an iced pole
until it stuck. And outside, or inside,
the first lights responded to evening,
and supper smelled to you sour as the odor
in the dark bedroom your parents said
was love each morning.

BANDING BATS

They are so delicate,
a woman's hands, gloved,
might not feel the small gag,
the lungs crushed by a nervous twitch.
So she works bare-handed
as they bite through her nails
and bring blood. She fears rabies,
like those tarantella dancers frenzied
with the dark bite of spiders.

There are other fears: the silent
treefalls crushing animals
on the trail, the emerald eyes
of spiders mirroring her headlamp,
working in jungle dark with the wrecked
flapping of netted bats.

Far away, she fears
she will never see her lover again,
nor her father who first held her in dark,
who brought her the first night-light.

Now a jungle guide teaches her how
a man driven with fever
twists a net-pole into damp earth,
captures a hundred bats a night,
piercing the rare ones with hypos—
a quick gust of air explodes the heart.

He tosses the common back into the dark,
shines light on the lifeless fur in his palm,
makes her a special offering.

Late at night
she returns to base camp and lies down,
sleepless. Was there wind alone
or the swish of a rotting tree
giving out at the roots?

Some hour later, she dreams of flying
to the civilized world, her loved ones
lit below like candles in a valley of fog.

But her body remembers, and brings her back:
she awakens with tight lungs, gags, drools,
feels the air whistling through her in a quick gust.
The light in her eyes snuffs out, and
something dark flaps far back in the brain.

TESTIMONY AT COURT HOUSE ROCK

for Ellesa

All of us hiked that day, hardly speaking.
Up Indian Staircase, toeholds held us
in the worn sandstone. At Court House Rock,
we inched up the stone flue
by the sheer press of our bodies against it.

Nothing but boulders below
and armfuls of air.
It's no wonder your legs gave out—
your husband already at the summit
locked in his solitude,
the rest of us oblivious as dust.

God damn it, I'm not stone, you cried.
Lend a hand, someone, lend a hand.

Though we all longed to breathe the higher air,
to hide our human scent in mountain pine,
those of us close by cooed to you,
as if calming a child, as if
the spoken syllables were guy lines
or pitons wedged safely
all the way to the top.

Later, at the summit, some of us
still listened to the wind in our ears;
others heard a more human voice.

OBEDIENCE

*Women are exempt from all of the positive precepts
related to time.*
—Talmud

We may commit suttee.
May carve our faces
with fine scars, paint
flesh with the clay
of our condition. We may
cast ourselves down in dust
or make ourselves less,
more beautiful for touching the earth
lightly in our tiny shoes,
the bones broken smaller.

If we rise, we may
stretch our necks with brass rings,
wavering on the brink of extinction
to please the suzerain.
We must stifle our screams
of pain or pleasure—
the long vowels and consonants,
partaking too much of time,
too long in the vanishing,
must not rise from the harem tent
into the night sky.

These precepts, hung
above earth like the blue dome,
we cannot touch. Like the sun
that rules forever,
marking the days and seasons
of our labor. To every sovereign
with the sun in his eyes,
we seem as shadows
bound to the earth,
our suppliant arms beautiful
as the limbs of bonsai.

SCAVENGING THE COUNTRY FOR A HEARTBEAT

WHIPPOORWILL

Where dark has fallen
it calls, closer
to your cottage door.

Wherever you turn, its song
compels you in three syllables
to open your door to the night.

You flash a beam into its red eye
and the goatsucker drags it in.
It holds its ground—

the last reserves of light die.
As you wish for more power
to dike the onrushing night,

whippoorwill takes flight,
his white wingbands slicing
a hole for you in the dark.

THE FAILING

I did not dream your death, but only mine.
—James Wright, "But Only Mine"

I have come home to search
the high grasses a last time:
cool and green willows once hung here,
now bulldozed lots blowing dirt
in sad pinwheels to Lancaster.

I remember listening for the song
of Mohawks who once bathed along these shores.
I must have fooled myself half a day
before the Nashua caked red-dye over the reeds—
the stink of sludge in every townsfolk
till they wanted to lash out, yank the slow mud
from these banks, and flatbottom it to Boston, to the sea.

All the muggy summers at the mills,
we were stained with 40-weight oil
and leaked our greasy rainbows into standing pools—
river-water severed from its source.
Now I rouse to remember
when my blood rebelled,
scavenging the country for a heartbeat.

You who remain, strain your ears
to the rhythm of wind over water—
the deeper pulse we seldom hear
here by the banks of the Nashua slowing
past blacktop, sluggish
with the roots of old,
upturned willows.

NORTH PLATTE TO CHICAGO, NOVEMBER NIGHTS, ROUTE 80

The lack of trees
makes no provision for the wind.
It speaks with one voice here:
moans across the prairie,
weathering keen-edged slate on farm roofs.

Through the windshield,
I feel the smallness of farm lights
set in the vast black onyx of plains,
the lone communication towers blinking
red radio light into the dark,
the gully bridges gripping the land together.

I click on the car radio.
Chicago is still blowing jazz
this late into the night.
Listening to Miles' muted trumpet,
I think he must be up with me,
letting the wind blow itself out through his horn.

Even this late, tower beams
carry across the fields of stubble,
the slow rising and setting of the land.
But by morning, their lights blink off
and I see the steel embedded in prairie soil.
Jazz fades to static, the spit emptied from the horn.

Outside the car, the outlines
of a silo, a farmhouse appear
across the plains, cemented there.
Tractors pull out from rows of stubble.
A few miles further on, another road
where they turn off.

I feel the roots that anchor them.
Maybe if I go past the speed limit,
I can outdistance the next night,
the next radio towers,
the wind.

IN THE NEVER SUMMER RANGE

for Jay

Glacial till trips us up in summer,
small evidence of a distant past
that froze mammals whole,
closed the buds of trees
to green eons later,
hugged everything
in a careful preservation.

Can we have carried with us, packed
along our mortal frames, memory
of this last snowmass,
winter that embraced us
more than the sun's promise?

Our hearts refuse fruition,
closing upon the bud of perpetual spring.
Here, winter stays with us year round,
topping the fencepost markings,
bowling over cairns,
until we could lose our way
and totter over a crevass.

Never Summer frosts the streams
in mid-August, keeps us dreaming
late in our tents. Never Summer
cools our daylight climbs,
turns sweat to ice at summit.

Never Summer, like the raven's rasp
from its stark branch as we ascend,
is the very air we pass through,
that passes through us, preserving us,
as at this altitude, petals tight with promise
will not open, sometimes, for fifty snowy years.

MISSION REEF

As a gift to the Florida Keys for saving its coral reefs,
the Italian government donated a forty-foot bronze
statue of Jesus.

Jesus wavers under water,
rooted to the coral reef,
his arms raised to welcome
or ward off.
                              His arms
bruised with fire coral,
fingers hung with sargasso,
gorgonia waving like snakes
about his ankles.
                              Anemones, medusa-eyes,
mottle his coppered flesh
with pocks and puckers,
flesh turning copper-green
in exotic water.

Barracuda brush his face,
moray wind his thighs,
grouper and midnight blue
harrow his body, algae-clothed,
nibbling it nub by nub.
No one would christen him now.

Drifting above him,
I see through distracted light.
Does he waver below me,
gesture me down to the green fire
of his arms?
                              Or has kelp and sea fan
woven about his face
become now like a new veronica?

ATCHAFALAYA NOVEMBER

We quiet the motor,
loop rope around a cypress stump,
and drift in the pirogue.

Snowy egrets circle out at dawn,
widening the compass of the known,
feel in their wings the fall sun
tensing the arrow of flight.
They arc a final time and are gone
along the flyways.

                        So we keep circling
and wait till the world rhythms reach us.
Cottonmouth sunning on logs, coral snake
tucked in a tree-cleft, long shadow of gar
gliding below: something in their leisure,
their slowing natures gathering
the last blessings of sun,
cause us to come ashore.
Knee-deep in mud, we pass
between their poisons brightening the earth.

For awhile, we are lost
and closer for having left the rest
of what we are, back there at the landing.
Here, the great oaks breathe our sorry exhalations
and give back to us the air purified of lament.
We hear each other's heart as one ripple
in the fabric of fall leaves,
and lift into the journey of dying with joy.
How long we go on dissembling our bodies,
with their notions of arms and legs, I can't say,
but sooner or later, the sound of highway,
rising on its pilings above the swamp, brings us back.

I notice your arms growing again from your shoulders,
your fingers budding out, feeling for your wallet.
Then, my arms and legs return.

I wind my watch. And we are back at the boat,
drifting in a dead-end inlet
while the fish jump for flies.
Our boat keeps bumping the cypress stump
saying *reduce* and *reduce*
again to this.

Soon we must give in
to the butterflies, like roses pinned to darkness,
landing on your hair and mine, give in
to the small tongues and tendrils
of the world that prey on us
with such tenderness.
Then we will look North
and hear it coming,
and not be afraid.

EVERGLADES

I wake to the swamp
and mayhem of a missing girl.
How did the father let her go,
his hand clutching at the emptiness?
How was it possible she dissolved
to nothing but a sleeveless dress
by the time rangers gutted the gator belly?
Down at the bottom of identity
I measure myself against the upcurved teeth,
whatever settles out of sight in the slime.

The Florida ranger pushes a life-
vest into my chest, says
Only one man I know
walked on water. The rest of us
muck about in this green scum.
Then he blue-pencils a route
to keep me afloat in late April.
And it occurs to me now, out here,
the canoe caught in mud and matted
grass, I trust the ranger more
than I trust myself. Now sawgrass
surrounds me. Wind slurs the rules
of what walks or wades.

I lean over the edge,
meet my face wavering
in a throng of fish.
Snakes slither off mangrove,
gar dart from the swamp bottom.
I blister and tire
half the afternoon
poling over thin inches of protozoan.
I've never dreamed so much life
in the space my shadow makes—
teeming life just in
a silhouetted head.

My paddle oozes up to the handle
and will not budge. The swamp has no bottom
I can see, kidney-colored, textured like intestines,
heaving a gasp and a suck
as I push my paddle in
and pull out.

And now I either sit and blister
or go over the edge
to haul the boat along.
Bottom comes. . . neither slight
nor solid. My legs thrash, root
to some wavering support.
The boat glides along on the thin edge
between water and water-life.
I plant again and push
into mud—or something
part mud, part dumb matter,
part gel of my leg.

THE BELL BIRD

(Matari Bay, New Zealand)

I smell lemon everywhere,
lemon-air and lemon-earth and lemon-trees
and long-leafed eucalyptus. When I arrive
at the canyon's rim and peer down a thousand

feet to the dusk-silent canopy of trees,
suddenly the Bell Bird sings.
Its song is almost human, a glissando
across the empty space. It wavers

on the edge of sunset, circling
along the rim or far down
in the gloom or far above
in the temperate air—it's impossible
to tell where the song comes from.

In the moment that lasts
until I am done hearing it,
the song goes on, solitary,
varied, with an uncertain refrain.

Time begins again when the song ends.
I record it faithfully, whistle
the first few phrases that will compose
themselves into a human tone.

They will rise and fall through the staves,
through the plaintive air, the opening
notes whistled by a voice not yet
a voice, a bell rung in the throat
of something that would be wild.

GIVING IN

(Rye Beach, New Hampshire)

Sunset we drive by sea marsh
where the northern harrier
hooks a shimmering fish.
A few rotting shacks
have given in to gravity,
their braces snapped,
jutting up.

Late summer, the littoral
dries to thigh-deep mud, and marsh gas
fills our heads with going.
Perhaps the summer birds
smell it as well. Something
makes them rise up and wheel
in longer and longer loops,
stretching south.

Cattails are losing their stuffing.
And beside them, the blackbirds laze.
No longer the furious chase
through willows, a crow's
caw always ahead of them.
Nothing's left to preserve.

For those who will remain,
mist glazes us with a briny cast
like salt-warped boards and green statues.
We are as permanent as
tonight's flaming moon
full above the fishing huts.

We could drive all night
preserving the salt on our lips
as rotting gases rise from the marsh,
or just park and let the moon come up
over the broken sheds.

ASTRONOMICAL

(Paxico, Kansas)

Shooting stars in Perseus,
luminous dust of creation,
come smoking out of the dark
and disappear as fast as we blink
back sleep. We watch from wheatfields
bits of planets exploding,
some astronomical number
of grain ripening in the dark.

Dimmer but more constant,
a satellite glints across the galaxy.
What speed to witness—
this man-wished thing
unbound from the earth's slow round,
sailing across the face of suns and moons.
What speed we ourselves move at—
846 miles per hour rounding the earth,
64,000 miles per hour around the sun,
and the galaxy turns on a center
north of Hercules, spiralling
43,000 miles per hour—as we drift
in and out of sleep in Kansas,
the grainfields ripening,
crickets pulsing, no wind.
The night, still.

FROM VANCOUVER, LOOKING WEST

Nimbus clouds rise from the horizon.
Enough sun before it dips into sea
to praise the fields of day.
If all endings were born of the same rose-infused light. . .
then a clear night and fallow tomorrow.

Pink evening
brightens the breast of a tern
as it goes down to nest.
I know, by a trick of memory, this light.
It bathed my beginning by the Maine coast
as it bathes me now. The same sky
lights the waters of both shores,

the same trajectory of gulls dipping for fish,
shells drop from the same height
to crack on a rock.
And each wave thins the land between,
for if there were the dream of a wave,
it would be to meet its undulant-other
at land's middle, to return to the days
of Creation, with land a mere prayer
not yet whispered out of the silence.

Tidal pools, here and there,
live and die in the moon's reflective
light—a glimmer from beyond
the earth's curve into darkness—
as night gathers us in.

WAKING UP, LOSING SELF

Just before dawn I break camp,
the others still in mummybags, mumbling good-nights.
As I cross a small crest,
the sun shivers through aspen,
dappled fossil-shade of leaves on my arms.

Higher still, pine needles give up
their brown breath, and the last scrubs
give way to the glint of mica.
Everything blends with birds
warbling me to treeline.

I shout out my name at the summit,
but it fails to echo
from the hard tongues of quartz,
long-ago white liquid song, cooled
and quiet now at timberline.
The birds too have abandoned me to silence,
to grub in the pines lower down.

While I still burn after the mossed-stone peak's
true North, the minerals in my blood begin running out of time,
drawn to magnets in mountains, to the lodestones in stars.

The whitest hairs half-asleep
in my body begin to sing
in the forest of my remaining years.

WARBLERS

Down low, yellow warblers *so-so-so-sweet*
in a wet spring of marsh marigolds and
downies drilling their meals from old oaks.
Up trail, wood sorrel reveal their pink inner
veins to a hiker's eye starved all winter
for color. Red stars of trillium against
green-ridged lobes, yellow bells of trout lilies:
these are the measures of his soul. But it is
the thirty-ninth year, the cline-edge where stripling
beech give way to blue spruce and hemlock, where black-
throated blue's ascending call gives way
to the mending note of slate-gray junco
or the old sorrow of white-throated sparrow:
how long can you live above treeline? Live
on obdurate granite and anemic veins
of quartz? Will you breathe the high air of thinning
circumstance, or return to the lush, mortal
swarm of mayflies, spring peepers, spring beauties,
that, in their confusion of hours, last
a lifetime: clutch, clasp, sting, and sing
all winter in our heads. Will you go down
and wait beside the springwood for the fall
dayflower, *comelina virginica* —
where each blue flower grows from a heart-
shaped spathe and glows, transfused, as night descends.

ANTHEM FOR THE DISEMBODIED

All morning wind has been droning
across the plains and grass unfurls
a gigantic prairie flag.
Guarding its tunnels,
the burrowing owl cackles on the fencepost
and warns me off to the next field.
In the next field the diamondback
hunts under the white sage
and wind blows shofar notes
through the holes of prairiedog skulls.

So you understand how it feels foreign
to the land, rootless as the amaranth in autumn—
the branching tips of tumbleweed splitting at the stem
are driven about in storm.
The rattler sheds skin after skin,
the owl disappears into a dark wind,
the skull into the black hole behind the eye
that takes us from the parting earth.

PLEIADES

Pleiades, the Seven Sisters, were companions of the goddess
Artemis. Amorously pursued by the giant hunter, Orion,
they were rescued by Zeus. He changed them into doves
(peleiades) *and placed them far off among the stars.*
—*Robert Claiborne,* The Summer Stargazer

Stars glitter in late September, each known constellation
seems clear and lucent as a planetarium sky. But
exceedingly far off, there's something like a smudge of light
to the naked eye. A more careful observer, field glasses
or telescope trained in that direction, might magnify
its meaning, extract from that dim cluster the beautiful
helix of stars winding upwards like the stuff of life
itself. Then Pleiades comes awake at an opaque

hour, reveals its rising swirl. All week, I've risen at three
a.m. for a glimpse of it. At this hour, Orion, too,
floats briefly over the southern rim, pursues the Seven
Sisters to their end. Invisible until near-dawn, now
he reveals his jeweled belt, his dagger, his heart clouded
by a great nebula. And at this hour, Pleiades' swirling
helix doubles in my lenses, my eyes blurred from too little
sleep, too little clarity in a come-cry without love.
The late-night whisper of space chafes at the unrest in my bed
where I have lain and looked at my lover as through the wrong
end of a telescope. Exceedingly far off,

there's more that bears witness. Last night,
I awoke to a single ring of the phone. China.
My American friend in trouble again, his voice
like a seafan wavering in deep ocean, the pressure
per square inch of Tiananmen Square and the latest purge.
His last letter, steamed open, returned to sender
along with Chinese translation. "I'm stuck in the Swan
Hotel, man, Room 802, take it down, I may never
make it out of this place. Too many people, man, you can't
believe the press of faces. My students have no heat. They dance

in their classes to keep warm, man. They gather around the
portable heater in my apartment and I feed them
vitamins. Man, I want to take a crowbar to my brain,
pry some light in. I can't connect the wires fast enough.
I'm so boringly brooding, man. Hit me with a white
light. Smoke my sockets. Give me my medicine of god-
forsakenness and godawful darkness. Man, I want
to humble myself to the heavens, sit on a thorn
until the world opens."
                    The phone crackles for awhile
like stars in late September, like dragon banners declare
majesty in a blustery sky. Then: "Man, I love you,
but gotta go. Room 802, man. Call a taxi. Steer
me home. I'll try to hold on." Then, a satellite's relayed
static, atmospheric, as I shout into the mouthpiece,
try to bring him back. Four operators—two English,
two Chinese—relay my words across time-zones, meridians,
light-sensitive. I talk louder as language becomes stranger:
Ni hao! Ni hao! Qing deng! And then, the Swan manager's
smoky voice: Very sorry. No answer in that room. *Zaijian!*

Three in the morning, I refuse the ready warmth of the bed,
her cursory questions readied for a man she barely
knows. I piss off the back deck, watch the first few inches
stream into invisibility, the Seven Sisters
swirling far off, and decline for the moment to magnify
them, bring them closer. Back inside, I settle into Woolf's
Mrs. Dalloway, her opaque yearnings for this day, hour,
moment, to be transformed beyond itself, and somehow
remain itself, the way mystery achieves a moment
of clarity before it goes dark. The planets lean close
outside my window, gleaming. But a few smudges of light
linger, so far off, they spiral down a staircase into
darkness, occluded by distance itself.